I0816548

# RUSSIA

BY SUE BRADFORD EDWARDS

Essential Library

An Imprint of Abdo Publishing
abdobooks.com

**ABDOBOOKS.COM**
Published by Abdo Publishing, a division of ABDO, PO Box 398166, Minneapolis, Minnesota 55439. 

Printed in the United States of America, North Mankato, Minnesota.
102022
012023

Cover Photos: iStockphoto (cathedral); Shutterstock Images (pattern)
Interior Photos: Helen Filatova/Shutterstock Images, 4–5; Shutterstock Images, 7, 18, 25, 35, 41, 73, 76–77, 80, 98–99; Lagutkin Alexey/Shutterstock Images, 8; V. Kuzmishchev/Shutterstock Images, 11; Starover Sibiriak/Shutterstock Images, 13; Andrei Stepanov/Shutterstock Images, 15; Elena Shchipkova/Shutterstock Images, 16–17; Peter Hermes Furian/Shutterstock Images, 19 (Russia); Web Tools/Shutterstock Images, 19 (globe); Nick Pecker/Shutterstock Images, 21, 28–29; Oleg Belyakov/Shutterstock Images, 22; Fufachew Ivan Andreevich/Shutterstock Images, 31; Vaclav Sebek/Shutterstock Images, 34; Mikhail Gnatkovskiy/Shutterstock Images, 37; Fine Art Images/Heritage Images/Hulton Fine Art Collection/Getty Images, 38–39; Universal History Archive/Universal Images Group/Getty Images, 43; Pictures From History/Universal Images Group/Getty Images, 45; Sovfoto/Universal Images Group/Getty Images, 47, 49; Vitalii Gaidukov/Shutterstock Images, 48; ITAR-TASS/AP Images, 51; Sergey Bezgodov/Shutterstock Images, 52–53; Alexander Zemlianichenko/AP Images, 54, 70–71, 72; Alexandra Harashchenko/Shutterstock Images, 57; Larysa Aleksieieva/Shutterstock Images, 58; Martynova Anna/Shutterstock Images, 59; Sefa Karacan/Anadolu Agency/Getty Images, 62–63; Roman Evgenev/Shutterstock Images, 64–65; Mikhail Klimentyev/Presidential Press Service/RIA Novosti Kremlin Press Service/AP Images, 68; Andrey Rudakov/Bloomberg/Getty Images, 78–79; Alexander Manzyuk/Anadolu Agency/Getty Images, 81; Konstantin Egorychev/Shutterstock Images, 83; Ewa Studio/Shutterstock Images, 86–87; Yury Kara/Shutterstock Images, 88–89; Education Images/Universal Images Group/Getty Images, 92; GTRES/AP Images, 94; Maximilian Clarke/SOPA Images/Light Rocket/Getty Images, 95; Nataliya Borysenko/Shutterstock Images, 101

Editor: Arnold Ringstad
Series Designer: Maggie Villaume

Library of Congress Control Number: 2022940382

**PUBLISHER'S CATALOGING-IN-PUBLICATION DATA**
Names: Edwards, Sue Bradford, author.
Title: Russia / by Sue Bradford Edwards
Description: Minneapolis, Minnesota: Abdo Publishing, 2023 | Series: Essential Library of Countries | Includes online resources and index.
Identifiers: ISBN 9781532199486 (lib. bdg.) | ISBN 9781098274689 (ebook)
Subjects: LCSH: Russia--Juvenile literature. | Europe--Juvenile literature. | Russia--History--Juvenile literature. | Geography--Juvenile literature.
Classification: DDC 947--dc23

# CONTENTS

CHAPTER **ONE**

# MEMORIES OF RUSSIA

It had been a few years since Anya's family vacationed in Russia, but the details were still vivid in her mind. The flight from New York City to Moscow, Russia, had taken an exhausting 15 hours. This included transferring from one plane to another in Belgrade, Serbia. After Anya's family checked in to their hotel and caught a quick nap, they took the Moscow Metro subway to Red Square to do some sightseeing.

Because Anya's father had grown up in Russia, he performed the role of tour guide. He explained that Red Square is the largest square in Moscow. He gestured expansively around the vast open space, which covers almost 800,000 square feet (74,000 sq m),

Besides being a popular tourism destination, Moscow's Red Square has been a site for protest demonstrations, military parades, and important speeches.

**In 2022, an estimated 12,640,818 people lived in Moscow.[3]**

and then toward the white, multistory Kremlin Palace.[1] A tall red brick building also stood on the square, as did a towering cathedral with brightly colored domes.

Anya's mother took over the narration. She noted that a kremlin is the fortress at the center of every medieval Russian city. This one is by far the most famous, she explained, so when people speak about the Kremlin, this is what they mean. It was built in 1490.

Next they walked toward one of the most iconic buildings in Moscow. Anya's father pointed toward the building with the colored domes and told her that this was Saint Basil's Cathedral. He said it was built under Tsar Ivan IV and completed in 1560. Each of the nine domes tops a chapel.

Anya's mother paid 2,100 rubles, about $30 in US dollars at the time, for the family to enter the cathedral that now serves as a museum.[2] Anya gazed at the bright icons, paintings of holy people bordered with gold, that hung on the walls. She looked upward at frescoes honoring the life of Saint Basil on the ceiling. In one of the cathedral's chapels, Anya peered around the sunlit interior of an elaborately decorated dome. Icons and metalwork were everywhere, including on many of the doors. Hanging in the chapels were massive chandeliers that helped illuminate the elaborate decorations. Each chapel was different. Some featured columns painted with vines or angels flying over arched doorways. In the Church of the Velikoretsky Image of Saint Nicholas, the dome's interior was unadorned white, in contrast to the surrounding splendor.

After leaving Saint Basil's, Anya and her parents located a café where they got lunch. Her father dined on transparent green cabbage soup called *shchi*. Her mother had thin pancakes folded into triangles. Anya noted that the pancakes looked different than those at home. Her mother explained that these pancakes, called blini, are made from buckwheat flour and often served with caviar. Anya was happy to be eating pelmeni. Her mother made the dumplings at home and served them with a sprinkling of fresh herbs, but Anya's had come with a dollop of sour cream.

After lunch, they entered the vast, multistory red brick building that was the State Historical Museum. When she saw that the displays were labeled in Russian, Anya was relieved her parents could translate for her. In the gallery devoted to the earliest people to live in Russia, Anya looked at pottery, a dugout boat, daggers, and spear points.

Room after room was full of coins, pottery, and paintings. Anya studied a covered sled that looked like a shed on skis. Her parents' favorite display was a model of a three-sailed naval galley complete with 20 oars on each side of the boat. By the time they finished touring the museum, Anya had

## SAINT BASIL'S CATHEDRAL

People refer to Moscow's nine-domed cathedral as Saint Basil's in honor of the Russian holy man who was buried at this location in the Trinity Cathedral, which burned in 1583. Construction of the new cathedral began the next decade under Tsar Ivan the Great, whose son added a chapel to honor Saint Vasily, or Basil, the Blessed.

**Weapons and armor from Russia's extensive military history are among the collections of the State Historical Museum.**

gained a much better understanding of the country's history. But she was also ready to see more of the actual country for herself.

At their hotel, Anya smiled when she saw Grandmother Anna hurrying across the lobby. Anya had been named after her grandmother. The name *Anya* is a different form of *Anna*. They went

### THE RAILWAY

Tsar Alexander III came up with the idea for the Trans-Siberian Railroad. He realized the benefit of being able to move goods and people from coast to coast. Construction began in 1891. One section was built eastward from Moscow and another westward from Vladivostok, with several others constructed in between. In 1904, it was completed, but the route ran through Chinese Manchuria. The tsar worried that if China fought Japan, the Japanese could seize Manchuria, cutting off Russian access to the railway. With the 1916 completion of another section, the railroad stretched from Moscow to Vladivostok within Russia, bypassing Manchuria. The railroad opened Siberia for settlement and extraction of its natural resources, including lumber.

into the hotel restaurant for dinner and ate a hearty soup called borscht, which was full of cubes of beetroot, ham, sausage, and beef. It came with sour cream and a chunk of hearty brown bread.

## TRANS-SIBERIAN RAILROAD

In the morning they gathered in the dining room for a breakfast of *kasha* and cups of tea. Anya liked the buckwheat breakfast porridge, but she shuddered when she saw her parents scooping fried onions onto their portions. After adding butter and a sprinkling of sugar to her own bowl, she met her grandmother's smile. Anya was glad to notice that she and Grandma Anna ate their kasha the exact same way.

After breakfast they caught their train. Anya was excited to ride on the Trans-Siberian Railroad to the Siberian city of Novosibirsk, where her grandmother lived. It would take 50 hours to travel 2,000 miles (3,219 km), and Anya wondered how they would occupy their time on the train.[4]

Grandma Anna showed the conductor their second-class tickets, and he pointed down the length of the car. A smiling attendant greeted them in Russian as they entered their compartment. There, Anya's parents stowed everyone's luggage on the high shelf above the door. When the attendant brought them bedding, Anya's father added it to the shelf. They took their seats facing each other.

"Where are the beds?" Anya asked.

"We're sitting on two of them," said her mother, who demonstrated how the seating folded down.

The compartment was hardly bigger than the beds, and Anya wondered about spending two days in the tiny space. She forgot these concerns as the train started moving and Moscow slipped past the windows. Soon they were traveling through the countryside. A short distance from the train rose an evergreen forest. The train swayed gently, and Anya dozed off.

When Anya awoke, Grandma Anna unzipped her suitcase, revealing granola bars, packets of kasha, chocolate, and four bottles of water. Anya needed to use the restroom, so her grandmother led her to the tiny shared restroom at the end of the train car. Anya was surprised when she flushed and the toilet simply opened to the track below.

**The Trans-Siberian Railroad stretches 5,778 miles (9,299 km) from Moscow to Vladivostok.[5]**

On the way back to their compartment, Grandma Anna showed Anya how to make tea at the samovar. This massive hot water kettle looked like a piece of factory machinery. Anya watched her fellow passengers make instant noodles, kasha, and tea.

The landscape was beautiful and green, but hour by hour it was much the same. Occasionally Anya spotted a river or a group of homes, but the landscape grew monotonous. Russia looked large on a map, but from the perspective of a train speeding along the ground it was even more massive than Anya had imagined. Periodically the train stopped at a town or village, and even if it was for only five minutes, Anya's family took the opportunity to walk outside in the fresh air.

At dinnertime, the attendant delivered four meals in square aluminum pans to their compartment. Each serving of buckwheat was topped by a piece of chicken. Four small boxes accompanied the hot dish and contained water, a package of cookies, a packaged piece of sausage, and a napkin. Afterward, Anya slept, and the next

**A journey along the entire length of the Trans-Siberian Railroad would take about eight days.**

day was more of the same. She was relieved when the train finally pulled into Novosibirsk and their long journey finally came to an end.

## ARRIVING IN NOVOSIBIRSK

The train station in Novosibirsk was a massive turquoise building with bright white trim. They took the subway to a stop near Grandma Anna's apartment, which was in a modern, multistory building. Once inside, there was a quick tour of the sunlit, two-room space with cheery orange cabinets.

Everyone wanted to spend time outdoors, so their first sightseeing stop was the zoo. They strolled through the wooded, parklike space. Anya's father provided a running commentary of facts and trivia, noting that the zoo held more than 11,000 animals.[6]

Grandma Anna pointed out animals native to Russia. These included the wolverine, bear, European otter, and roe deer. Anya's favorite was the mighty Siberian tiger. In addition to the animals, the zoo featured many sculptures, snack stands, and birdhouses.

### NOVOSIBIRSK

Novosibirsk developed after the Trans-Siberian Railroad was built. Located on the Ob River, the city has thrived because of the nearby Kuznetsk coalfield, and it is now the largest city in Siberia. It is a center for food processing and plants that manufacture military aircraft, mining machinery, agricultural machinery, and consumer goods, including pianos, knitwear, and shoes. With Novosibirsk State University and other educational institutions, Novosibirsk has among the highest proportions of students in advanced education of any Russian city.

**Novosibirsk is home to many institutions of higher learning, including Novosibirsk State University.**

On the way back to the apartment, the family stopped at the Central Market. Bigger than a school gymnasium, the busy building was full of stalls selling dried fruits, spices, mushrooms, meat, and fish of all kinds. Back at the apartment, the family made a traditional Siberian meal. It included *gruzdyanka*, a potato and mushroom soup, along with fish rolls called *gruzinchiki*. Grandma Anna promised that the next time Anya visited, they would pick mushrooms in the forest.

A few days later, Anya and her parents flew back to Moscow and then caught their flight back to New York. It had been an amazing journey. Anya knew there was much more to see, and she wanted to return before long, but rising international tensions made travel to Russia much more challenging now. Glancing through her scrapbook of photos from the trip, she hoped that one day soon she would be able to visit Grandma Anna in Russia again.

## A VAST AND DIVERSE NATION

The Russian Federation, more commonly known as Russia, is the largest country in the world. It spans 5,600 miles (9,000 km) from Europe in the west to the Pacific Ocean in the east. Russia is more than twice the size of the world's second-largest country, Canada. It encompasses 11 percent of the world's land and stretches across 11 time zones.[7] Politically, it is divided into 86 republics, territories, and districts.

Given Russia's impressive size, it is no surprise that the country is so varied. The people come from more than 100 ethnic groups and speak more than 100 languages.[8] With this diversity of cultures, the nation also has many different cuisines, styles of dress, and art forms. The geography includes mountains, forests, and wide grasslands.

Russia faces serious challenges today. Its leader, President Vladimir Putin, has launched military attacks on neighboring countries, most notably Ukraine in 2022. His government has also jailed or even killed political opponents and critics. These actions have caused Russia to become more and more isolated in the international community.

Wildflowers bloom on the Siberian landscape overlooking the Anadyr River, one of a seemingly limitless number of incredible natural and cultural sights that visitors can experience in Russia.

CHAPTER **TWO**

# GEOGRAPHY

Russia is by far the largest nation in the world, encompassing about 6.6 million square miles (17 million sq km).[1] Stretching across the continents of Europe and Asia, it is bordered by three oceans: the Arctic in the north, the Atlantic in the west, and the Pacific in the east. The country's varied landscape includes frozen coastlines, vast plains, and towering mountains.

Two mountain ranges and a highland region have shaped the country's geography. Western Russia's Ural Mountains run from north to south. In southern Russia, the Caucasus Mountains extend roughly from the northwest to the southeast and divide the country from Southwest Asia. Within the Caucasus, the highest point in Russia, Mount Elbrus, soars to an

The Ural Mountains in western Russia form the border between Europe and Asia.

elevation of 18,510 feet (5,642 m).[2] In eastern Russia, the Kamchatka Peninsula is a highland where 127 volcanoes, 22 of them still active, created a series of mountains.[3] Mountains and highlands alike create high-altitude geography where the temperatures drop with each foot of elevation. Western Russia is generally more mountainous than eastern Russia.

Russia is a country rich in lakes and rivers, with some estimates for the number of rivers being as high as 100,000. Russia's five longest rivers are the Ob, the Yenisey, the Lena, the Amur, and the Volga. Located in Siberia, the longest river is the Ob at 2,268 miles (3,650 km). With its headwaters in the Altai Mountains, it drains into the Arctic Ocean. The largest city on the Ob is Novosibirsk. The Yenisey River is 2,167 miles (3,487 km) long. It begins in Mongolia and empties into the Arctic Ocean. It has the seventh-largest drainage system in the world, covering about 996,000 square miles (2,580,000 sq km). The Lena River begins near Russia's Lake Baikal and runs 2,734 miles (4,400 km) before emptying into the Arctic Ocean. There are

### MOUNT ELBRUS

The tallest mountain in Europe and a part of the Caucasus Mountains, Mount Elbrus is an inactive volcano. The mountain is covered with snow year-round. In July and August, climbers from around the world visit and attempt to reach either the east or west peak. High winds, heavy snow, and the high elevation make it a dangerous climb, and approximately 15 to 30 climbers die on Mount Elbrus each year.[4]

# MAP OF

# RUSSIA

**KEY:**

- Capital
- City
- Point of Interest

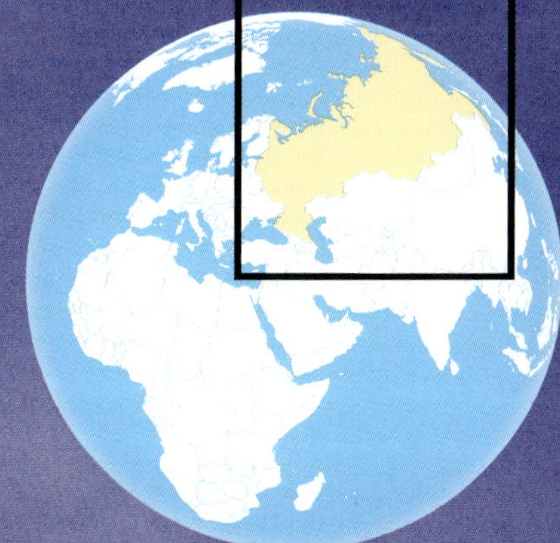

many nature preserves within its vast delta. The Amur River flows 1,755 miles (2,824 km) and crosses territory in Mongolia, where it is called the Kharamuren, and China, where it is called the Heilongjiang. The Volga, Europe's longest river, runs approximately 2,193 miles (3,530 km) from northwestern Russia into the Caspian Sea.[5]

Among Russia's many lakes are the two largest lakes in Europe. Lake Ladoga is near the city of Saint Petersburg and is the largest lake located entirely in Europe. It has a surface area of 6,864 square miles (17,700 sq km). Europe's second-largest lake is Lake Onega, with a surface area of approximately 3,820 square miles (9,894 sq km).[6] It lies in Russia's northwest.

## TUNDRA

Russia's northernmost biome is the Arctic tundra, a polar desert that is frozen much of the year. The annual precipitation is less than 10 inches (25 cm), and the biome has extremely cold temperatures. The average winter temperature is –30 degrees Fahrenheit (–34°C). On average, only six to ten weeks of the year have warm enough temperatures and enough sunlight for plants to grow. During the summer, typical temperatures range from 37 to 54 degrees Fahrenheit (3–12°C).[7]

**Russia's coldest recorded temperature was –90 degrees Fahrenheit (–68°C) on February 6, 1933, in Oymyakon, Siberia.[8]**

Because of the extremely cold temperatures, tundra soil is largely permafrost, meaning it is permanently frozen. Even during the warmest time of the year, only the shallow top layer of soil thaws.

The Russian tundra features enormous expanses of flat land and temporary lakes created by thawing permafrost.

The Perm region of Russia, near the Urals, is home to vast stretches of taiga.

Plant roots can grow only within this thawed soil, which is why the tundra lacks trees. Without deep roots to anchor them, any trees would be blown over by the region's high winds. The lichens, sedges, mosses, grasses, and small shrubs found in the tundra remain low to the ground and grow quickly.

Tundra animals must also adapt to the cold temperatures and to life in an area with a short growing season. Some have evolved heavy fur coats to stay warm and reduce their bodies' energy use, while others store fat as an energy source. Others hibernate, sleeping through the coldest winter temperatures, and some species migrate or temporarily leave the area, returning only when temperatures rise and food becomes more abundant.

## FOREST BIOMES

There are two different forest biomes in Russia. Just south of the tundra is the taiga. *Taiga* is a Russian word meaning "marshy pine forest." The permafrost and layers of rock that underlie the soil mean that the ground is wet, boggy, and poorly drained. This creates expanses of shallow bog known as muskegs that deceptively resemble solid ground. Mosses and grasses can grow on the surface of the water, but beneath this layer of plants the ground is spongy and wet. The cool, wet climate means that mosses, mushrooms, and lichens thrive.

Rising above the boggy ground are the coniferous trees that give the taiga its name.

**75 percent of Russia's land is composed of taiga.[9]**

Conifers, trees that produce seeds enclosed within cones, dominate these forests. Taiga conifers include the larch, which is a Russian conifer that sheds its needles in winter, and several varieties of evergreens. Evergreens, including Siberian cedar trees, shed only some of their needles each year. The heavily forested taiga contains the world's largest supply of timber.

Summers in the taiga are short, mild, and humid. Summer temperatures in July are generally around 50 to 55 degrees Fahrenheit (10–13°C). Winters are cold and snowy, with temperatures usually dipping well below freezing. Some of the coldest areas in Russia are in the Siberian taiga.

The second forest biome in Russia is the broadleaf or deciduous forest. This forest receives more rainfall than the taiga, so it can support trees with larger leaves. Broadleaf trees' wide leaves allow more water to evaporate from them compared with conifers. Because of this, these trees require more moisture than conifers do to thrive. East of the Ural Mountains, a band of birch and aspen trees separates the taiga from the next biome to the south, the steppe.

## LAKE BAIKAL

Lake Baikal is located in southern Siberia between the taiga and the steppes. It is the world's largest lake by volume and the world's deepest lake. It covers 12,248 square miles (31,722 sq km) and reaches a maximum depth of 5,577 feet (1,700 m). By comparison, North America's Lake Superior has a maximum depth of 1,332 feet (406 m).[10] Lake Baikal holds 20 percent of the world's fresh water. There are 27 islands within the lake, including Olkhon, an island that is 45 miles (72 km) long. During the winter, the lake can freeze to a depth of 6.6 feet (2 m).[11]

Large areas of steppe are found in a broad belt across southern Russia.

## STEPPE

Steppes are open grasslands, but there isn't a clean dividing line between forest and steppe. Instead, in the southern woodlands, stands of birch and aspen are interspersed with areas of grassland. Moving farther south, the grassland becomes more abundant and the trees scarcer until they can be found only around rivers. The principal plants in the steppe are grasses such as bunchgrass, fescue, and bluegrass. These are short grasses, few growing higher than 20 inches (50 cm) due to the limited rainfall.[12] Lichens and mosses also thrive in this open region that is hot and dry in the summer and cold in the winter with little snow. Because of the low rainfall, the steppe is classified as semiarid, and few trees grow in this biome.

The steppe includes areas of gently rolling hills and flat-bottomed lakes. Large rivers, including the Ural, and their tributaries cross the steppe. *Chernozem*, or "black earth," is the Russian word for the soil of the steppe. The upper level, often more than three feet (1 m) deep, is rich in humus because winter cold and summer drought keep plant matter in the soil from decaying or being carried away.[13] This makes the soil incredibly rich and fertile, explaining why this is a key grain-growing region in Russia.

## ICE AND COLD

The climate of any given geographic area is impacted by its latitude. Latitude is the distance that a place is from Earth's equator. Places that are near the equator generally have warmer climates compared with places farther from the equator. This is because at the equator the sunlight is strong and direct, while near the poles it strikes the planet at an indirect angle. Altitude is another factor that determines how warm a given area is. Higher altitudes mean lower temperatures.

Russia is much closer to the North Pole than it is to the equator. There are also extensive mountains and plateaus. Taken together, these two factors give Russia a cold climate. That is

### THE POLAR NIGHT

Because it is in the far north, the Russian tundra experiences a phenomenon known as the polar night. During winter in Russia, Earth's Northern Hemisphere is tilted away from the sun. Because of this tilt, as Earth rotates throughout the day, the northernmost areas of the planet never move into sunlight and experience no sunrise. The Russian town of Murmansk goes 40 days with no sunrise in winter. Residents of Murmansk celebrate the first sunlight of the year, gathering at a local mountain to experience about a half-hour of sunlight before the sun sinks below the horizon.

why, despite its extensive eastern coastline on the Pacific Ocean, the country has few ice-free ports. Vladivostok, located on the Sea of Japan, became part of Russia in 1860. It is the nation's only port that is ice-free the whole year. This is made possible using ice breakers, ships that create a channel through ice and keep the port open to shipping. Cold weather and ice have made transportation throughout Russia difficult, impacting not only shipping but also the ability to build and maintain highways and travel by road. During the winter, some areas in the far north go days without sunlight, experiencing the polar night.

CHAPTER **THREE**

# PLANTS AND ANIMALS

Each of Russia's biomes is home to plants and animals that have adapted for life in this part of the world. In the tundra, soil is scarce and low in nutrients. Paired with the region's cold temperatures and short growing season, this limits plant life. The word *tundra* is from the Sami people who settled Finland; it means "treeless." Mosses grow well in this biome. They grow slowly and require few nutrients, helping them survive the harsh winters.

The tundra is an important breeding ground for a variety of birds that migrate into the region for the short summer season. One of these is a species of duck known as the spectacled eider. While on the tundra,

The red-throated loon, found in Russia's north, is brownish-gray as a juvenile and gains its distinctive neck coloring as a breeding adult.

spectacled eiders feed in shallow water, seeking seeds and insects. They winter on the Bering Sea, swimming in gaps in the ice and diving for clams. Other seasonal residents include wading birds, the curlew sandpiper, the sharp-tailed sandpiper, the broad-billed sandpiper, and the red-throated loon. Like other loons, the red-throated loon is a diving bird, but it is smaller and can also catch fish midflight.

A bird that lives on the tundra year-round is the willow ptarmigan. This compact member of the grouse family has adapted to life on the tundra with feather-covered feet that allow it to walk across freezing snow. In the winter, the bird digs burrows in the snow as protection from brutally cold winds. It also displays seasonally appropriate colors to improve its chances of survival—white in the winter and a mix of red and brown in the summer.

Another tundra animal that displays seasonal color changes is the arctic fox. In the summer it is gray or grayish brown, and in the winter it is blue-gray or white. The fox lives inland from the ocean and is an opportunistic hunter, eating fish, birds, and small rodents such as lemmings.

One of the largest animals on the tundra is the reindeer, the only species of deer with both males and females growing antlers. An adult male can be as tall as 4.4 feet (1.3 m) at the shoulder and 6.8 feet (2.1 m) long. Females are smaller, reaching up to 6.2 feet (1.9 m) in length.[1] The reindeer's hooves are among its most important adaptations because fur on the bottom of the hooves keeps the animal from slipping on icy ground. In addition, the edges of the hooves are sharp, which helps the reindeer dig down to reach plants even in the winter. In the summer, the reindeer's broad hooves help it paddle as migrating herds swim across lakes or rivers.

Prey is harder for the arctic fox to find in winter, so it sometimes scavenges the leftovers of kills made by larger predators, such as wolves or polar bears.

Human activities threaten the tundra. Mining, especially for gold and tin, have polluted the water and destroyed aquatic areas that used to teem with fish. Arctic waterways connect European and Asian ports, and these shipping lanes may see increased use if exploration discovers oil, gas, or other important resources in the region. An oil spill would be hazardous for wildlife living in this fragile ecosystem.

### REINDEER

Reindeer are wild animals that have been domesticated. The Nenets people of northern Russia are a tribe of reindeer herders who depend on their reindeer to survive. Reindeer pull the sledges that haul people and gear, the animal's meat provides food and is sold for income, and reindeer hides are sewn into clothing and tentlike shelters called *chums*. The Nenets also saw off reindeer antlers and export them to buyers in China, where the powdered horns are sold as traditional medicine for men.

## FOREST WILDLIFE

Just as the plants and animals of the tundra are suited for that environment, those that live in the taiga have evolved to thrive in this forested biome. The region doesn't have the rainfall to support broadleaf trees, so instead the evergreen trees here evolved thin leaves called needles. These evergreens include fir, pine, spruce, and cedar. These slender leaves have a waxy coat, which, along with their limited surface area, reduces water loss when dry winds blow across the landscape. The branches of these trees do not reach up toward the sky but bend downward so that snow slides off instead of building up and snapping off branches. The trees also grow close together, which adds protection during a heavy snowfall.

## A PINE MYTH

Some people believe that other plants won't grow near large evergreen trees because pine needles are acidic, but tree and gardening experts know this is not true. Pine needles are slightly acidic when they drop off the tree. But even if the needles immediately turned into soil, the acidity level would be too low to harm plants. One reason it is hard to grow other plants under and around evergreens is that evergreens have shallow root systems that compete with other plants for surface water and nutrients. Evergreens also create a lot of shade, which makes it hard for plants below them to grow. Fallen needles form a dense blanket of ground cover that blocks even more sunlight.

Because these evergreen trees do not shed all their leaves in the winter, they don't use much energy growing new leaves in the spring.

The region is home to several large mammals, including what may be the most well-known Russian animal: the Siberian tiger, also known as the Amur tiger. It is one of the largest big cats in the world, with males weighing 353 to 419 pounds (160–190 kg) and females 243 to 287 pounds (110–130 kg).[2] These tigers are adapted to life in the cold. They have longer, thicker coats than other tigers, as well as extra fur on their paws and a fluffy ruff around their necks. Large animals such as tigers need a lot of calories to survive, especially in the cold, and Siberian tigers eat wild boars, deer, and the occasional brown bear. The most serious threat to this big cat is illegal hunting, which is driven by demand for its body parts in traditional Chinese medicine.

Other large animals in the taiga include brown bears, lynx, wolves, various deer species, and wild boars. Wild boars are highly adaptable and live in a variety of habitats, including

Siberian tigers typically live and hunt alone as adults.

the taiga forest. These animals range in size from 1.8 to 3.3 feet (0.6–1 m) tall and 5 to 7.9 feet (1.5–2.4 m) long. They are omnivorous, eating seeds, roots, fruit, eggs, insects, and carrion, or dead animals. They live in groups of six to thirty animals wherever vegetation provides cover from predators.[3]

### BAIKAL SEAL

In Russian, the Baikal seal is called the *nerpa*. It is the only seal that lives exclusively in fresh water, and it is small compared with other seals. It feeds on both fish and plankton known as amphipods, tiny crustaceans that are less than half an inch (10 mm) long. Like the seals, these amphipods live only in Lake Baikal. A seal can catch more than 50 amphipods per dive.[4] The seals have evolved specialized teeth that help them filter their prey out of the water while swimming.

In addition to large animals, the forest provides a home to many smaller animals, including hares, ermines, otters, squirrels, moles, and birds. A wide variety of seed-eating birds migrates to the area during the summer when food is plentiful, but they do not reside in the taiga year-round. These birds include goldfinches, chaffinches, siskins, waxwings, and starlings. Other birds come to the taiga during the summer to dine on the mosquitoes and other insects that flourish in the warm, wet months. These birds include warblers, flycatchers, and woodpeckers. Predatory birds, including owls and eagles, live in the taiga year-round, eating voles, hares, and a variety of rodents.

The climate grows warmer south of the taiga. Interspersed with the evergreens are deciduous trees including birch, aspen, oak, ash, hornbeam, and maple. Farther south, deciduous trees increase in number until they are more common than the evergreens. The forests transition to broadleaf, not taiga. Birch and aspen are the most common deciduous trees east of the Ural Mountains. Many of the animals in this broadleaf forest are the same as those in the taiga.

## STEPPE PLANTS AND ANIMALS

Steppe plants are adapted to withstand drought, fire, frost, and grazing by the saiga antelope and other steppe animals. Plants that thrive on the steppe include turf plants, such as feather grass, timothy, and bluegrass. Another common steppe plant is the tumbleweed.

Many of the animals that live on the steppe shelter in burrows. Among these animals are ground squirrels, voles, lemmings, marmots, pikas, and hares. One of the larger steppe animals is the saiga antelope. The saiga antelope is about the size of a goat, weighing 51 to 88 pounds (23–40 kg) and standing 25 to 31 inches (63–80 cm) tall at the shoulder.[5] These animals graze on grasses, onions, shrubs, and other plants. Scientists are unsure how many of these animals live in the wild. This is in part because starting in May 2015, a mass die-off occurred, and some 200,000 of them perished throughout Russia, Mongolia, and China.[6] Scientists eventually discovered the cause was blood poisoning by bacteria. Saiga antelope are

**The saiga antelope has been considered critically endangered since 2002.[7]**

also threatened because their natural steppe habitat has been fragmented by agriculture, making migration difficult.

Agriculture is also a threat to the native plants that grow on the steppe. Instead of native grasses and herbaceous plants, farmers grow rye, oats, and corn. There are also non-grain crops such as sugar beets, which are not eaten as a root vegetable but used as a source of sugar. Agricultural fields no longer support native plants and animals.

**Saiga antelopes have an unusual bulbous nose that scientists believe evolved to filter out dust in the summer and warm up cold air in the winter.**

CHAPTER **FOUR**

# HISTORY

Historians believe that the ancestors of today's Russians arrived in the area around 500 CE. They were Scandinavian peoples who moved south from modern Norway, Denmark, and Sweden. These people eventually settled around the Volga River. Here they mixed with people from the western Slavic ethnic group and built a fortress that became the Ukrainian city of Kyiv. These people became known as the Rus, and by 972 they had expanded their territory as far north as modern Saint Petersburg and as far east as Moscow. Vladimir the Great ruled Kyiv from 980 until 1015, and today both Russia and Ukraine claim him as their founder.

By 1054, the Rus kingdom was in decline largely because of the invading Mongols. Ancestors of today's

An 1822 painting depicts the decision of Vladimir the Great to make Christianity the religion of his kingdom in 988.

Tatar peoples, the Mongols raided Kyiv and the surrounding Rus territories 156 times from 1450 to 1647. Under this assault, the territory fragmented, and Moscow became the center of Rus culture.

### TSAR OR CZAR

The Russian language is written in a script called Cyrillic, which differs from the Latin script used for English and many other languages. As a result, the English spelling of translated Russian terms can vary. In the English alphabet, the term for a Russian leader has been written as czar, csar, tsar, and tzar. Different spellings have been popular in different English dialects and at different times. Similarly, the city of Kyiv, which is the capital of Ukraine, was commonly spelled Kiev when Ukraine was part of the Soviet Union. Kiev is the Russian preference, popularized during the time of the USSR. Kyiv is the Ukrainian preference, and it has become the version most often used in the West today.

## THE TSARS

Even before Kyiv was on the decline, Moscow was on the rise. It started as a small fur trading center, but the nobles who ruled there expanded their territory by conquering their neighbors. In 1300, Moscow controlled approximately 7,722 square miles (20,000 sq km). This domain broadened to 166,024 square miles (430,000 sq km) by 1462 and 2.1 million square miles (5.4 million sq km) by 1584.[1]

One of Moscow's nobles, Ivan IV, was crowned Tsar of all the Russians in 1547. In addition to conquering territory, the new tsar developed a standing army that he used to briefly push back the Mongols. He developed a parliament and a council of nobles to help him rule. He also oversaw the construction of Saint Basil's Cathedral. Other landowning nobles were below the tsar and his family in the social structure. These nobles also helped lead the military.

**The fear inspired by Ivan IV led to his common nickname in English: Ivan the Terrible.**

In 1558, Ivan launched the Livonian War (1558–1583) in an attempt to take the land that is now Latvia and Estonia. Ivan took part of the territory, but several nobles supported his enemies. Angered by their disloyalty, Ivan created a military secret service that gathered intelligence on suspected traitors and executed those it found guilty. Members of this secret service were known as the oprichniki.

The next major tsar was Peter I. His father, Tsar Alexis, died in 1676 when Peter was four. Peter's older half-brother was named tsar, but he died in 1682. Peter and another half-brother were named joint tsars. A series of family members ruled on behalf of the brothers, but there was constant conflict until Peter's brother died and Peter took over in 1696. The continual struggle among ruling factions meant the leaders' focus had been on gaining power, not developing the country's industry and economy. As a result, Peter ruled a Russia that lagged behind neighboring nations. To fix this, he recruited western European advisers and encouraged the development of a middle class focused on trade. He developed industry and metallurgy so Russia could manufacture its own armaments and ships and build up a military. Using this military, Peter took Estonia and Latvia from Sweden in the Great Northern War (1700–1721). He died in 1725.

The tsars built Russia into an empire, but not all Russians benefited. The nobles controlled the land and the serfs. Serfs were farmers and laborers forced to remain on the land where they were born. Each year, the serfs had to give the nobles part of their crop or work in the nobles' fields. They couldn't leave if an area experienced famine, and they were also the only people drafted into the military.

Even when the tsars tried to improve the lives of the serfs, they often did too little. Tsar Alexander II came to power in 1855 and quickly decided reform was essential to keep Russia moving forward. In the Emancipation Manifesto, issued in 1861, he freed 20 million serfs, but they received only small plots of land to farm and had to make large payments to their landlords, the nobles.[2] His military improvements were more effective. Nobles could now be drafted during war, and punishment using physical force was forbidden. But those who wanted reform didn't think he was doing enough, and a revolutionary terrorist group assassinated him in 1881.

## WORLD WARS AND THE COLD WAR

Russia's last tsar was Nicholas II. He led Russia into the disastrous Russo-Japanese War (1904–1905). Long after it was obvious that Russia couldn't win, Nicholas insisted that his military continue to fight. Thousands of Russian troops died. The Russian people demanded changes, and protests ranging from student marches to labor strikes occurred across the country. On January 22, 1905, a protest march to the Winter Palace in Saint Petersburg led to the Russian military killing more than 100 demonstrators.[3] This event, which became known as Bloody Sunday, led to more worker strikes, unrest among the peasants, and military revolts. To quell the violence, Nicholas agreed to the October Manifesto, a document that created a constitution, a multiparty government, and

**An elaborate ceremony marked the coronation of Tsar Alexander II. The wealth on display was a stark contrast to the poverty of Russia's millions of serfs.**

the state Duma, or legislative body. Nicholas failed to take the reforms seriously and passed laws to return himself to absolute power.

In the next decade, Russia entered World War I (1914–1918), coming to the aid of its allies France and England against Germany. The Russian Army was not equipped to fight a lengthy war, and it took heavy losses. In September 1915, the Duma demanded reform. Nicholas discontinued the legislative session and went to assume command in the field. This left his wife, the tsarina, in charge alongside her principal adviser, a self-made holy man named Grigori Rasputin. The tsar's actions and the tsarina's reliance on Rasputin left the nobles certain that they had to be replaced.

### THE TUNGUSKA EVENT

On June 30, 1908, at about 7:14 a.m., a massive explosion occurred at 28,000 feet (8,500 m) when an asteroid 120 feet (37 m) across blew up in Earth's atmosphere above a remote part of Siberia. Forty miles (64 km) from the explosion, the force of the blast knocked a man off his chair while on his front porch at Vanavara, a Siberian trading post. In 1927, an expedition led by Leonid Alekseyevich Kulik, chief curator of the Saint Petersburg museum's meteorite collection, found the epicenter of the blast near the Podkamennaya Tunguska River. His discovery was aided by a ring of approximately 80 million fallen trees circling the blast site.[4]

The Duma wasn't alone in demanding change. Striking workers and other citizens took to the streets to protest the war. In March 1917, the tsar ordered the military to fire on protesters, but the soldiers joined the protests. When police began shooting protesters, fighting broke out. On March 14, the Duma formed a provisional government, and the tsar and his son were dethroned. The next year, the tsar and his family were executed.

Approximately 1.8 million Russian troops died in World War I.

The provisional government did not have unanimous support, and multiple groups fought for power. Eventually the Bolsheviks, a political party under the leadership of Vladimir Lenin, overthrew the interim government and formed a new communist nation called the Union of Soviet Socialist Republics (USSR), also known as the Soviet Union. Lenin and his supporters wanted to correct the flaws of the tsarist system, especially the widespread poverty and the concentration of wealth in the hands of only a few people. Following Lenin's death in 1924, Joseph Stalin took over leadership of the USSR. Stalin worked to build up the country's industrial strength. At the same time, he launched purges against those he perceived as disloyal, killing or imprisoning millions of people in the 1930s.

Another world war came to Europe in 1939. Germany, led by Adolf Hitler and his Nazi Party, invaded Poland and started World War II (1939–1945). Stalin did not want to get involved in a war against Germany. Weeks before Hitler's invasion, the USSR signed a peace pact with Germany. And weeks after the invasion, the USSR also invaded Poland in its own separate interests. In the meantime, the nations of western Europe battled the Nazis. But in the summer of 1941, Germany turned on the USSR, launching a surprise invasion. German forces broke through the first line of Soviet defenses, but their offensive stalled before reaching Moscow. By this time, winter had begun to set in. Unequipped for the cold weather, the Germans

**The Soviet Union sustained approximately 24 million total military and civilian deaths during World War II.[5]**

Some of the most iconic images from World War II include photos of Soviet troops raising their flag over the ruins of the German capital during the closing days of the Battle of Berlin.

were steadily pushed out of Soviet territory over the next few years. Millions of troops died on each side. In April 1945, Soviet troops launched a bloody battle for the German capital, Berlin. At the end of the month, with Stalin's forces closing in from the east and American and British troops approaching from the west, Hitler shot himself in his bunker in Berlin. Germany surrendered in early May, ending World War II in Europe.

As the conflict ended, the situation between the Soviet Union and its wartime allies worsened. Leaders of the USSR said the United States and the United Kingdom had not been quick enough to offer support as they fought the Nazis. The USSR also wanted to retain control over the parts of Poland that Germany had seized during the war. It set up a Soviet-aligned government for Poland and drafted Polish citizens into the Soviet military.

This convinced Western powers, especially the United States, that the USSR and other communist countries sought to expand their influence across the globe. This belief and a mutual distrust led to a fierce rivalry between the United States and the Soviet Union. This confrontation became known as the Cold War. The two sides never fought each other directly, but they competed for international

## SPUTNIK

On October 4, 1957, the Soviet Union launched Sputnik 1 into space. This satellite, the first artificial object that humans launched into orbit around Earth, was the size and shape of a beach ball and weighed about 184 pounds (83 kg).[6] Once every 98 minutes, the satellite completed an orbit around Earth, sending out a beeping signal. This signal could be picked up on Earth, and the satellite could be seen at night by the naked eye. The Soviet accomplishment triggered the space race, an intense competition in the field of space technology. In another important achievement, the Soviet Union launched the first person into space on April 12, 1961, sending pilot Yuri Gagarin into orbit around Earth before returning him safely to the planet.

# VALENTINA TERESHKOVA

Valentina Tereshkova was born in the village of Maslennikovo on March 6, 1937. She began working in a textile mill at age 18. She also took correspondence courses from an industrial school and became skilled at parachuting from airplanes. In the early 1960s the Soviet space program called up four women, including Tereshkova, to undergo training for a space mission. On June 16, 1963, she launched into space aboard Vostok 6.

Tereshkova became a symbol of USSR space achievements, appearing in public and traveling abroad. She later attended the Zhukovsky Air Force Engineering Academy, earning a degree in technical science in 1976. She went on to hold roles in the government of the Soviet Union. In 2011, she was elected to the Russian Duma.

On Vostok 6, Tereshkova made more than 40 revolutions around Earth in a flight lasting nearly three days.

prestige and in the development of nuclear weapons and space technology. The two sides also spied on each other and produced propaganda to promote their own worldviews and interests.

Tensions remained high in the 1980s as Soviet leader Mikhail Gorbachev sought to improve the economy. The nation's farms seldom produced enough food, and shortages of vital goods were frequent. In late 1990, the government collapsed, and economic reforms were put into place. In 1991, the Soviet Union formally dissolved.

## FRAGMENTATION AND EXPANSION

The Soviet Union's dissolution created 15 independent nations, including Russia, Ukraine, Latvia, Lithuania, Estonia, and Belarus. Russia's first president, Boris Yeltsin, ushered in a new age. The government was no longer controlled by the Communist Party, and people could vote for members of the government. Private businesses arose, and people from minority ethnic groups revived cultures that had been suppressed under the communist regime. Yeltsin was reelected in 1996 but resigned due to poor health in 1999. He selected the country's prime minister, Vladimir Putin, to replace him as president.

In 2000, Putin won the presidential election to remain in office. He removed cultural freedoms supported by Yeltsin and took control of the national television networks, giving the government control over news and other programming. Putin was reelected in 2004. The Russian constitution states that the president can serve only two terms in a row, so Putin was legally unable to run in 2008. Instead, Putin became prime minister and supported the election of a loyal aide, Dmitry

**Vladimir Putin, *left*, has been the most powerful man in Russia since taking over the presidency from Boris Yeltsin, *right*.**

Medvedev, as president. Medvedev won, and he changed the presidential term to six years, to take effect during the next president's term. Medvedev declined to run again, and Putin won the presidential election in 2012, though with less popular support than before. When people protested the elections as unfair, they were arrested and imprisoned as traitors.

In 2014, Putin ordered the Russian military to move into Ukraine's Crimean Peninsula after a widely disputed election where Crimea's population voted to become part of Russia. Ukraine and the international community condemned this action, but Russian forces remained in the area. Putin signed an agreement with Crimean leaders to make Crimea part of Russia.

CHAPTER **FIVE**

# PEOPLE AND CULTURE

More than eighty percent of all Russians have Slav ancestry.[1] Although Russian is the country's official language, a variety of ethnic groups speak more than 100 other languages. The most common minority language is Tatar, spoken by approximately 3 percent of Russia's population.[2] The ancestors of the Tatars were the Mongols who invaded Russia and pushed the Rus people toward Moscow. The Tatars were once nomadic, and they are still known for traditional foods that sustained them when traveling, including horse meat and hearty baked goods. Their best-known dish is *chak-chak*, a dessert of fried bread and honey.

Cultural festivals help people celebrate and preserve traditional Russian clothing and customs.

The Bolshoi Ballet was founded in 1776, making it one of the oldest ballet companies in the world.

Ukrainian is another minority language. The Ukrainian language and culture are distinct from Russian, although each has influenced the other. Officials in Kyiv estimated in 2018 that approximately three million Ukrainians lived in Russia.[3] As early as tsarist Russia, the Ukrainian language was forbidden and was not taught even in Ukrainian schools. In modern times, people from minority ethnic groups have tried to preserve their languages. In September 2012, Chuvashiya in western Russia began a campaign to preserve the Chuvash language. But a 2018 Russian law limited how many hours schools could spend teaching minority languages.

## THE ARTS

Russia has a strong artistic heritage that includes both classical music and ballet. Perhaps the most well-known ballet company in the world is Moscow's Bolshoi Ballet, based at the Bolshoi Theatre. Also famous, and a rival of the Bolshoi, is the Mariinsky Ballet in Saint Petersburg. Both companies perform around the world and employ top foreign dancers. However, following Russia's 2022 invasion of Ukraine, many of these dancers left and international performances were canceled.

One of Russia's most well-known classical composers is Pyotr Ilich Tchaikovsky. Born May 7, 1840, Tchaikovsky could speak and read Russian, German, and French at age six, but his passion was music. By the time of his death in 1893, he had written three ballets, nine operas, and many other works, including the *1812 Overture*. He is most well-known for his ballets—*The Sleeping Beauty*, *Swan Lake*, and *The Nutcracker*—which are still performed today.

Russia is also known for its literature. Its most famous authors are Leo Tolstoy and Fyodor Dostoyevsky. Tolstoy wrote realistic fiction, including the novels *War and Peace* and

### BABA YAGA AND THE FIREBIRD

Russian literature includes folktales about Baba Yaga. Depending on the story, Baba Yaga may take the form of a forest spirit, a wise old woman, or a witch. What the stories have in common is magic and a clear warning to respect nature and elders. Another series of folktales involve the *zhar-ptitsa*, or firebird. This magical bird with golden feathers and crystal eyes drops pearls from its beak when flying over poor villages so that the people have something to trade for food. Anyone who carries a firebird feather is said to be protected.

*Anna Karenina,* which are both still widely read in literature classes. Dostoyevsky was a novelist and short story writer who explored human darkness in his novels *Crime and Punishment* and *The Brothers Karamazov.*

Perhaps the most recognizable art from the Soviet era is the propaganda poster. Governments use propaganda to communicate a specific point of view and rally citizens to a national cause. In the Soviet Union, the government encouraged patriotism and urged people to meet work goals. The posters included striking, stylized images that grabbed people's attention and encouraged them to make sacrifices for what was considered the greater good.

## CUISINE

Russian cuisine varies regionally, but there are several staple foods. A typical quick breakfast is an open sandwich with one slice of rye bread, butter, cheese, and a slice of *kolbasa* sausage. Hot cereals include semolina and oatmeal. Eggs are not scrambled but eaten fried along with kolbasa, tomato, or bell pepper in an omelet. Other breakfast options include *syrniki*, or cheese dumplings, and pancakes called blini.

The main meal of the day is often lunch, which is typically served between 1:00 and 2:00 p.m. Ideally this is a multicourse meal with soup, the main dish with a fruit drink, and tea with a sweet dessert. Common soups are *shchi*, made with cabbage and meat, borscht, made with beets and meat, and mushroom soup. Main dishes generally feature a meat and a starch, such as beef stroganoff with mushrooms. Other dishes include *kotlety*, which are flat, oval meatballs served with

**Blini are often served with jam, honey, or sour cream.**

mashed potatoes, *tefteli*, which are meatballs cooked in tomato sauce, and pelmeni, which look like tortellini. *Kompot* is a fruit drink made by boiling water with berries and then adding sugar.

In such a vast country, there are numerous regional specialties. For example, Siberian cuisine includes dishes that rely on local foods such as mushrooms, edible ferns, fish, and game meats, such as grouse, deer, and bear. There are also fish dishes, such as gruzinchiki and *stroganina*, which is sliced frozen fish with salt, spices, onion, and vinegar.

## SPORTS

Given the country's climate, it isn't surprising that many of Russia's popular sports are suited for cold weather. One of the most popular is ice hockey, which spread across the USSR following World War II. One legendary coach, Anatoly Tarasov, created a Russian style of play that combined a hard physical game with precise skating. He led the Russian team to Olympic gold in 1964, 1968, and 1972. Ice hockey remains popular, with Russian athletes playing on teams worldwide.

Ice-skating is also popular, with children taking lessons at figure skating schools. They learn to skate forward and backward and on one foot. Skaters learn to brake and how to fall on ice. Figure skating and speed skating are both widespread. Famed Russian figure skaters include Anna Shcherbakova, who won a gold medal at the 2022 Winter Olympics in Beijing, China.

Cross-country skiing is another common recreational activity. Historically, it is how people in the countryside got from place to place when it was too snowy to walk or bike. The Soviet Army even made use of cross-country skiing against the Nazi invasion in 1941, using skis to move tens of

### GORODKI

One uniquely Russian sport is *gorodki*. A group of wooden cylinders, called gorodki, is stacked in one of 15 named patterns including cannon, star, crankshaft, lobster, and sickle. The object of the game is to throw a wooden bat to topple the gorodki. Players have up to four attempts at bat per turn, and they throw the bat in slightly different ways depending on what pattern has been used. In 2009, gorodki became available in video game form on the Nintendo Wii.

thousands of Soviet troops into position. Many students today take cross-country skiing as part of their physical fitness classes.

Biathlon is a sport that combines cross-country skiing with target shooting. After World War II, the Soviet government held sports festivals named after athletes who had died in combat. Many people competed in biathlon at these events, which stressed the importance of both fitness and border defense. By the time the USSR dissolved, the biathlon was widely televised, and audiences watched athletes from Russia compete against those from other European nations, including Germany, Norway, Sweden, and Ukraine.

Not all Russian sports involve snow and ice. Weight lifting, gymnastics, and boxing draw many spectators and athletes. So do games such as basketball, soccer, tennis, handball, volleyball, and rugby.

**In 2012, Russian biathlon athletes trained in Sochi, Russia, ahead of the 2014 Winter Olympics in the same city.**

## HOLIDAYS

The Russian people observe a wide variety of holidays, including Maslyanitsa. It is the oldest Russian folk holiday and celebrates the end of winter. Throughout the week, round cakes symbolizing the sun are served with butter, caviar, nuts, and honey, as well as a variety of fish-based side dishes.

Christian holidays are also celebrated in Russia, including Easter and Christmas. In the Catholic Church, Christmas is celebrated on December 25. In the Russian Orthodox Church, it is celebrated on January 7.

One popular political holiday is Defender of the Fatherland Day, celebrated on February 23 each year. Schools and many businesses close, there are military parades, and traditionally gifts are given to men and boys to honor their obligatory military service. As more women serve in the military, they too have been included in the holiday.

International Women's Day is celebrated on March 8. Businesses are closed, so beforehand male coworkers and employers give women flowers, candies, perfume, or cosmetics. Male relatives give wives, mothers, daughters, and sisters cards and small gifts, often celebrating with a festive meal and champagne.

Russia Day, celebrated on June 12, became a public holiday in 1994. It commemorates the declaration of Russian sovereignty in 1990, but at first many refused to celebrate because it was also a reminder of the Soviet Union's collapse. Now people celebrate the successes of their fellow Russians on this day. It is a day off work, and people attend concerts and watch fireworks.

## RELIGIONS

More than half of the people in Russia are Christian, and most of these Christians follow the Russian Orthodox Church. Like other Christians, Orthodox Christians believe in God, Jesus, and the Holy Spirit and celebrate sacred rites including marriage, communion, and baptism. But there are also unique elements to how they practice their faith, including the icons that play a central role in worship. These beautiful paintings on wood often have a gold leaf background. Images depict Jesus, his mother Mary, saints, or Bible stories.

Islam is the next most common religion, with 10 to 15 percent of Russians belonging to this faith.[4] Many Muslims live in the states of Tatarstan, Bashkortostan, and the North Caucasus. Significant populations of Muslims live in the cities of Moscow, Saint Petersburg, and Yekaterinburg.

Another religion practiced in Russia is Tengrism, which has been revived as part of a movement to revitalize Central Asian cultures. Genghis Khan brought Tengrism to the Mongol people in the

### USSR ANTI-RELIGIOUS CAMPAIGN

Joseph Stalin and other Soviet leaders believed that religion was not compatible with communism, so they worked against religious organizations. In the 1920s and 1930s, their principal target was the Russian Orthodox Church. Clergy were killed, believers were sent to labor camps, and churches were closed. By 1939, only 500 of approximately 50,000 original churches remained. During World War II, Stalin revived the church as a source of anti-Nazi nationalism. By 1957, the number of active churches rose to 22,000 before the Soviet Union once more turned against religion.[5] Russia experienced much greater religious freedom after the collapse of the Soviet Union.

Russian Muslims gathered in Moscow to pray on the holiday of Eid al-Fitr on May 2, 2022.

1200s CE, although many later became Muslim. The chief god is Tengri, the infinite, timeless sky god. Believers also worship Yer-sub, the Earth goddess, and Erlik, the god of the underworld. Tengrism has spirits of land, water, and earth, as well as ancestor worship.

**There were more than 5,000 registered religious organizations in Russia in 2017.[6]**

CHAPTER **SIX**

# POLITICS

The Russian Federation is made up of 85 administrative divisions called federal subjects. There are multiple categories of federal subjects, including republics, oblasts, *krais*, *okrugs*, and federal cities. There are 22 republics, many of which correspond to a minority ethnic group. Among them are Chechnya, Tatarstan, and Dagestan. Republics are also called states, and each has its own constitution and legislature, called a duma.

Although each republic is autonomous in some matters, the Russian constitution always takes precedence. In 2010, a federal ruling stated that the chief executives of these republics would no longer be called presidents, a term reserved for the head of the federation.

A large building in the federal city of Moscow, known as the White House, serves as the headquarters of the Russian government.

An oblast, sometimes called a province, is a region that consists of a city and the surrounding area. There are 47 oblasts in Russia, and most of them, including Tyumen and Arkhangelsk, are named after their cities. One exception to this is the Jewish Autonomous Oblast in Russia's far east.

There are nine krais within the Russian Federation. A krai can also be called a frontier or a territory. Historically they were on the frontier, the boundary between Russia and a neighboring country. The people who live in a krai are often not ethnically Russian. Krais have the same status as oblasts and include Kamchatka and Stavropol.

There are four okrugs. These autonomous areas are created around ethnic minorities and are usually part of an oblast. Because of this, they do not have their own constitutions. Khanty-Mansi and Yamalo-Nenets are both okrugs within the Tyumen oblast.

Three federal cities are also part of the federation. A federal city consists not only of the city itself but also of nearby towns and other nearby cities. The two oldest federal cities are also two of the largest cities in Russia—Moscow and

### THE JEWISH AUTONOMOUS OBLAST

The Russian name for the Jewish Autonomous Oblast is Birobidzhan. This administrative division was established on the Soviet-Chinese border in 1934 with Yiddish as its official language. The government gave people train tickets to travel there, but they arrived and found crudely built barracks, poor land for farming, and no roads. By 1936, Stalin's government was persecuting Jews for speaking their language and practicing their religion even in this remote oblast where they were never the majority. Today, only a tiny fraction of the oblast's people are Jewish.

Saint Petersburg. The most recent federal city is Sevastopol, which is one of the contested areas in Crimea. Though it is under Russian control, the international community still recognizes it as Ukrainian territory.

## THE GOVERNMENT

**In 2022, approximately 5,432,700 people lived in Saint Petersburg.[1]**

Russia's form of government is known as a semipresidential federation. This means that there is an elected president, a prime minister, and a cabinet which together form the executive branch of the government. The president appoints the prime minister, so they are both from the same political party. He or she also appoints the governors that are the highest executive officials in the oblasts and frontiers. The president leads cabinet meetings and gives orders to the prime minister. The president can also veto any act or law passed by Parliament and is the commander in chief of the military.

The prime minister serves as the president's deputy and has many administrative duties. He or she nominates cabinet members and government ministers for the president to approve. The prime minister implements government policy within Russia, disciplines members of the government as needed, and carries information between the president and other parts of the government. This person represents Russia at government functions and meets with foreign officials.

The Russian constitution includes authority over the nation's military as one of the powers of the president.

Parliament is Russia's legislative branch and consists of two houses. The upper house is the Federation Council, which is composed of 170 appointed seats. The lower house is the State Duma of 450 elected seats. Parliament creates legislation.

The Judicial Branch includes a Supreme Court, which is the highest court in the land, and a Constitutional Court. Judges are nominated by the president, which gives the president a great deal of authority over how the courts work. Prosecuting attorneys and defense attorneys appear before a judge, and juries are seldom part of a trial. Because defense attorneys are so expensive, people charged with a crime often have no representation.

The Russian government has a reputation for being corrupt, and many politicians have no tolerance for criticism or dissent. Alexander Litvinenko was a former Russian spy who defected to the United Kingdom in 2001. He remained a critic of both the Russian government and Putin, and he was investigating Russian crime organizations when he got sick in 2006. After he died, the British authorities discovered he had been poisoned by a radioactive material called polonium-210. Investigators traced the polonium-210 to a specific nuclear reactor in Russia, but they had no definitive proof linking the Russian government to Litvinenko's death.

## POLITICAL PARTIES

Although 31 Russian political parties were registered in 2022, only eight had seats in the legislature. These include A Just Russia – For Truth, Civic Platform, Communist Party of the Russian Federation, Liberal Democratic Party of Russia, New People, Party of Growth, Rodina, and United Russia.

Formed in 2001, United Russia is the country's largest political party. It had two million members in 2017.[2] It is also the party of President Vladimir Putin. It is a conservative party focused on strengthening the nation's military and making sure that young people receive what is considered a patriotic education. In 2011, United Russia maintained a majority in the legislature. However, it no longer had the two-thirds majority that had allowed it to make changes to the constitution during the previous session, when it lengthened the presidential term from four years to six. Within days of the 2011 election, 5,000 complaints had been filed concerning unfairness in the election process.[3]

When Putin was reelected president in 2012, the legislature passed new laws so that anyone who protested without permission could receive a large fine. In addition, any nongovernmental organizations that received money from outside of Russia had to file as foreign agents. People who have criticized Putin or the United Russia party have been persecuted by the government.

Lawyer and protest organizer Alexei Navalny reports on Russian political corruption and frequently criticizes Putin directly. He has described United Russia as the party of crooks and thieves. He cannot run for office because he was twice convicted on fraud charges for

Supporters of the Communist Party continue to celebrate controversial figures from the Soviet era, including Joseph Stalin.

**Russian security forces cracked down harshly on protests against Alexei Navalny's imprisonment in early 2021.**

## THE TWO-HEADED EAGLE AND THE BEAR

The coat of arms of the Russian Federation includes a two-headed eagle. It first appeared on the seal of Ivan III in 1497. The seal was used to press this symbol into sealing wax whenever the tsar produced an official document. The bear is another Russian symbol. Starting in the Middle Ages, bears appeared on many European maps of Russia because mapmakers thought of Russia as dangerous, wild, and unruly, like a bear.

supposedly stealing $500,000 worth of lumber from a state-owned business.

In 2020, while traveling in Siberia, Navalny got sick and slipped into a coma. He was transported to Germany, and doctors found he had been poisoned by a nerve agent in his tea. After recovering, he freely returned to Russia. Soon after, Russian authorities arrested and detained him. He was sentenced to more than two years in prison. In 2022, the government added nine more years to his sentence.[4] Navalny is widely viewed as a victim of political persecution.

## POLITICAL SYMBOLS

When Tsar Peter I modernized Russia, he built up a fleet of ships. These ships needed a clearly recognizable flag, and the tsar chose a flag of white, blue, and red. His choice may simply have been a matter of rearranging the stripes on the flag of the Netherlands, which is red, white, and blue, but the colors have since been given Russian meanings related to the shield of the Grand Principality of Moscow. The shield itself is red, and depicted on it is Saint George in a blue cloak on a white horse.

Under the Soviet Union, a new flag was chosen. It consisted of a red banner with a gold hammer and sickle crossed in the upper left corner and a five-pointed star, outlined in gold, above them. The red banner was chosen because during the French Revolution, a plain red flag became a symbol for the rights of the people. The hammer stood for the workers and the sickle for the peasants. The gold star above these two figures symbolized the ultimate communist goal of global victory. When the USSR was disbanded, this flag was replaced with the earlier Russian flag.

## THE COLLECTIVE SECURITY TREATY ORGANIZATION

The Collective Security Treaty Organization (CSTO) is a military mutual defense alliance of Russia, Belarus, Armenia, Kazakhstan, Kyrgyzstan, and Tajikistan. Its goal is to preserve the territories of the member countries and to seek cooperation with other organizations, including the North Atlantic Treaty Organization (NATO) and the United Nations (UN). Like the UN's peacekeeping forces, CSTO maintains a rapid-reaction force that Russia contributed 8,000 troops to in 2021.[5] These troops are intended to aid member allies if they are invaded.

Just as the flag needed to be replaced following the dissolution of the USSR, so did the national anthem. During the Soviet era, it had been the "State Anthem of the Soviet Union," composed by Alexander Vasilyevich Alexandrov in 1944. Its replacement, "The Patriotic Song," was used from 1991 until 2000 but was unpopular. It was replaced in 2000 with Alexandrov's melody and slightly reworked lyrics in a song now called "State Anthem of the Russian Federation."

**Russia maintains a military of approximately 850,000 service members.[7]**

## MILITARY

After the dissolution of the Soviet Union, Russia had to decide how to update its military. In the 1990s, President Boris Yeltsin told the population that he planned to modernize the military, downsize it, end conscription, and increase soldiers' pay, but very little actually changed. Each military unit is composed of a core of trained soldiers with other roles filled, as needed, by conscripts.

The Russian military consists of three branches—the Ground Forces, the Navy, and the Aerospace Forces. Russia's forces include thousands of advanced tanks and combat aircraft. It exports many of these vehicles to other militaries throughout the world. The country also has a large arsenal of nuclear weapons, which can be delivered by land-based missiles, submarine-launched missiles, and bomber aircraft.

Russian forces include a mixture of professional volunteer troops and conscripts. The country has two drafts per year, one in the spring and one in the fall, and annually drafts approximately 260,000 men.[6] About half of these men are instructed to report to their local *voenkomat*, the offices that organize newly drafted soldiers and send them on for training. These new conscripts have one to two months of basic training before they move on to another one or two months

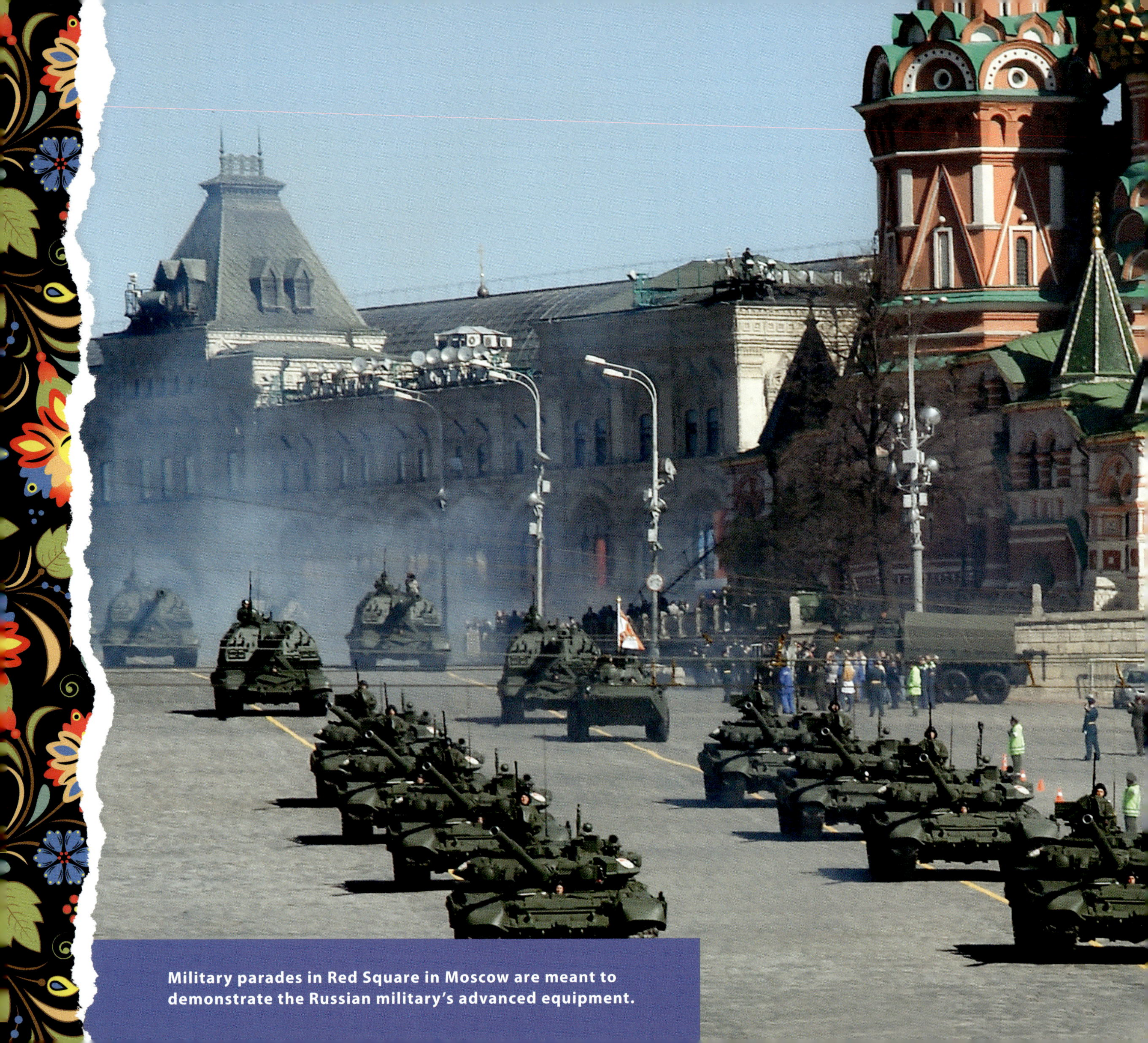

Military parades in Red Square in Moscow are meant to demonstrate the Russian military's advanced equipment.

of specialized training. They are then sent to their assigned units. Russian law states that no one can be sent to combat with less than four months of training, though emergency mobilization in the event of war could require this. Conscripts serve for a period of one year. Professional soldiers sign a service contract and serve in elite units, such as the airborne units.

Although they cannot be drafted, women can volunteer for military service. In World War II, women served as snipers, infantry soldiers, and combat pilots. Women in Russia's military today do not serve in combat roles but work as cooks, administrative support troops, radio operators, and medical staff.

CHAPTER **SEVEN**

# ECONOMICS

Approximately 67 percent of Russia's workers are employed in the service sector. This portion of the economy makes up 56 percent of the country's gross domestic product (GDP), which is the monetary value of all goods produced and services provided within the country.[1] The service sector encompasses any companies involved in providing services, including such diverse areas as hotels, catering, entertainment, and construction.

Another vital part of Russia's economy is its natural resources. These resources include oil, natural gas, aluminum, gold, gemstones, iron, coal, palladium, titanium, and uranium. Palladium is used to make jewelry, dental fillings, electronic components, and

**Russia has long produced titanium alloys for use in the world's aerospace industries.**

catalytic converters for cars. Titanium is a metal that is as strong as steel but lighter in weight, making it useful in building aircraft, bicycles, ship hulls, submarines, golf clubs, laptops, crutches, and other objects where weight is an important factor. In the form of titanium oxide, it is used in house paint, paper, and sunscreen, as the titanium blocks harmful ultraviolet light from reaching the skin. Uranium is used as fuel in nuclear power plants.

## INDUSTRIES

A wide variety of industries play a part in Russia's economy. Russia's leading industry is machine building, which has important centers in Moscow, Saint Petersburg, the Urals, and western Siberia, as well as around the Volga River. This industrial sector builds the machinery used in other industries and involves agricultural equipment, electric generators, and the construction of ships, aircraft, tanks, and trains. Vehicles made by Russian arms companies are also exported to other countries.

### EXPORTS AND IMPORTS

Russia's principal exports include crude oil, refined petroleum, and petroleum gas, which is used for heating, cooking, and producing hot water. Other leading exports are gold and also coal briquettes used to heat homes. In 2020, Russia was the world's largest exporter of wheat and nonfilleted frozen fish.[2] Russia's primary imports include car parts, cars, broadcasting equipment, packaged medications, and computers. Russia's key trade partners have been China, the United States, the Netherlands, Belarus, Germany, South Korea, and Italy. Following Russia's invasion of Ukraine in 2022, many countries limited or blocked Russian imports as part of economic sanctions.

**Enormous pieces of machinery are used to extract coal in Russia's open-pit mines.**

Another leading industry is fossil fuels. In part, this is because this sector is responsible for producing the energy that keeps other industries going. Significant oil and coal resources mean that Russia is a major exporter of energy. The only country in the world that produces more electricity than Russia is the United States. Some of that power is exported to other countries, but Russia itself is the third-largest consumer of electricity in the world.[3]

Also vital are Russia's chemical industries. Manufacturing synthetic rubber and chemical fertilizer in the early 1900s was important to Russia's industrialization. These industries continue today, and Russia also manufactures resins and plastics. Still, the chemical industry in Russia is not as diversified as it is in the United States, Canada, China, or the countries of the European Union.

Metallurgy is an important component of Russia's economy. This includes smelting and refining mined ores, as well as producing roll stock, which is also known as sheet metal. Iron and steel make up the bulk of Russia's metallurgy industry by volume, but more income is generated by other metals, such as copper, zinc, lead, nickel, aluminum, and titanium. Also important are precious metals such as gold, silver, and platinum.

Agriculture is another major Russian industry, especially large-scale agriculture. There are 850,000 square miles (2.2 million sq km) of agricultural land in Russia.[4] Farmers grow crops such as sugar beets, sunflowers, potatoes, and flax. Other leading crops are grains, including rye, wheat, barley, oats, corn, millet, and rice; as well as legumes, which include peas, beans, soybeans, and lentils. Russia's grain and legume production is fourth in the world after China, the United States, and India.[5] Dairy, meat, and wool are also key products of Russian agriculture.

## RUSSIA'S AGRICULTURAL RANKING

In 2021, the United Nations Food and Agriculture Organization estimated that Russia's agricultural capacity could feed two billion people. In 2019, Russia was the world's largest producer of barley and the third-largest producer of wheat. It was also the largest exporter of wheat. It was the second-largest producer of sunflower seeds and the third-largest producer of potatoes and milk. The country was the sixth-largest producer of eggs and chicken meat.[6]

## CURRENCY

The primary unit of Russian currency is the ruble. In 1704, Peter I minted the first silver ruble coins. In modern Russian currency, 100 kopecks equal one ruble. Kopecks come in denominations of one, five, ten, and 50, although one- and five-kopeck coins are rare because they are of so little value. Ten- and 50-kopeck coins each have an image of Saint George killing a dragon. They are made of brass or steel coated with brass. The ten-kopeck coin is yellow brass and the 50-kopeck coin is red brass. There are also ruble coins valued at one, two, five, and ten rubles. The front of the coin has its value and an abstract design, while the reverse has a two-headed eagle and the value written out. The one-, two-, and five-ruble coins are made slightly differently, but they all have a silver color. The ten-ruble coin looks golden but is made of brass-coated steel. Paper banknotes are available in denominations

**Russia introduced banknotes in 200-ruble and 2,000-ruble denominations in 2017.**

**In May 2022, one US dollar was equal to about 65 Russian rubles.[8]**

of five, ten, 50, 100, 200, 500, 1,000, 2,000, and 5,000 rubles.

Following Russia's invasion of Ukraine in early 2022, many countries levied harsh sanctions against the Russian economy. The value of the ruble dropped sharply. But within a few weeks, it had rebounded to about the same value it had before the invasion. This wasn't because the sanctions failed but because the Russian government manipulated the value of the ruble. The ruble supply was limited because of banking sanctions, and by raising demand for the ruble, it increased in value. Russia did this by forcing Europeans who bought Russian energy to pay for it with rubles. This meant that the Europeans first had to convert their currency into rubles. In addition, Russian exporters who earned foreign currency were forced to exchange 80 percent of their earnings for rubles.[7] These steps by the government increased demand for the ruble and drove up its value.

## TRANSPORTATION ACROSS RUSSIA

Travel in Russia involves moving goods and people across huge distances. Most rivers flow north and south, which limits their use in moving goods east and west. Russia's climate also makes it difficult to maintain road safety in cold, icy weather. Because of this, materials and people often move over great distances by train. Air travel is much faster, and passengers often choose this route if they can afford it.

## OLIGARCHS

Under the Soviet Union, the government owned factories and other industrial facilities. When the Soviet Union collapsed, people scrambled to take control of these valuable assets in the new, more open economy. Many of these people had previously regulated the industries they now controlled, including energy and mining. They amassed enough wealth and power to influence the Russian government, making them even richer and more powerful. These business leaders have become known as oligarchs. Among them are Vladimir Lisin, who made his money in steel, and Leonid Mikhelson, whose fortune comes from natural gas.

Following the dissolution of the Soviet Union, more people and goods have been transported by car and truck as people earn more money and can afford to buy these vehicles. In winter, when lakes and rivers freeze, people drive across the frozen surfaces and use them as temporary roadways. In areas with permafrost, drivers must stick to paved roads because permafrost turns to mud under the pressure of a vehicle. This also means that building roads and railroads on permafrost is costly, slow, and difficult. Travel during spring thaw can also be treacherous because a vehicle will most likely get stuck in the mud.

One issue with travel in Russia is that much of the transportation infrastructure was developed during the Soviet era. By the time the Soviet Union went into decline, money was lacking and maintenance became less frequent, leaving infrastructure in poor condition. Many Russian roadways are still in need of repair.

People also have to get from place to place within Russia's cities, but during the Soviet era little emphasis was placed on personal transportation. Few people had cars, so they took buses

Some stations on the Moscow Metro include features such as chandelier lighting, engraved arches, Stalin-era mosaics, and beautiful stained glass.

or the subway. Only six cities, including Moscow, Saint Petersburg, and Novgorod, have subway systems. People continue to take subways, buses, and trams wherever possible because these modes of transportation continue to receive a government subsidy that started under the Soviet Union. This government money keeps the fares artificially low. The Moscow Metro is the world's busiest subway system, serving 8.5 million riders a day.[9] It was built in 1935. Transportation can be tricky for visitors because train and metro signs are posted only in Russian. To sound out a place name, visitors must know the Cyrillic alphabet.

**Russia has 576,459 miles (927,721 km) of paved roads and 221,001 miles (355,666 km) of unpaved roads.[10]**

CHAPTER **EIGHT**

# RUSSIA TODAY

Daily life in Russia varies based on where a person lives. In Moscow, getting to work involves dealing with heavy traffic, so commutes by car may take as long as an hour. Metro trains are punctual, but train lines and stations are not always conveniently located, and trains are crowded. In their free time, people like to shop, go skating, or attend soccer games.

People in different cities do similar jobs, but the demand for certain skill sets varies according to local industry. In Moscow in 2022, there was a high demand for people in information technology, business development, finance, human resources, and the

Families in Moscow enjoy shopping, dining, and spending time among their city's beautiful buildings.

In 2022, the estimated life expectancy for a Russian man was 66.9 years. The life expectancy for a Russian woman was 78.3 years.[1]

medical and pharmaceutical industries. In Saint Petersburg, employers were looking for sales professionals, drivers, and engineers. The typical workweek in Russia is 40 hours long.

While their parents are at work, young people spend the day in school. Education in Russia begins with primary school, which lasts four years starting at age six or seven. Next is basic general, which is the following five years, and secondary education, which takes two or three years. Secondary education may be at a general school or a vocational school. Students study topics such as the Russian language, literature, foreign languages, Russian and world history, economics, law, geography, physical education, math, and technology.

There are two types of vocational schools in Russia: professional schools and professional lyceums. Professional schools prepare students for particular jobs, so their education focuses on the skills students need for those jobs. At a professional lyceum, students study for a profession but also take general educational classes to help them prepare to enroll at a university. At the end of secondary education, students must pass the Unified State Exam to enter college.

## RECREATION

Russian city dwellers like to spend time in the country at a dacha, or cottage. Not all dachas are small and quaint. One dacha might be two humble rooms. Another might be a house with two

### THE UNIFIED STATE EXAM

The Unified State Exam was first administered to students in 2001. Like a high school exit exam, it tests students on the Russian language, mathematics, and other subjects. Officials hoped the Unified State Exam would reduce bribery during the university application process. The Levada Center, a Russian research institute, reports that bribery still occurs. Students sometimes look for exam questions ahead of time, use cell phones to look up answers, or receive assistance from those administering the exam.

stories and three bedrooms. A wealthy Russian may have a large and ornate mansion for a dacha. In the summer months, many Russians leave behind city apartments to spend weeks in the countryside.

During the Soviet era, dacha gardens were essential. Food shortages meant that the tomatoes and other produce people could grow in the country were necessary to feed their families. Today, these same gardens are a way for people to unwind and spend time with their hands in the soil. Gardens aren't the only source of fresh food. People also hike in nearby woods to forage for berries and mushrooms.

In some Russian families, someone lives year-round at the dacha and keeps chickens or even goats. Other people visit every weekend except in winter. Children swim in nearby lakes, and in the evenings families play board games, dominoes, and chess.

Cold weather doesn't necessarily keep Russians indoors. In the cities, people ice-skate at public rinks, including one in Red Square. At Lake Baikal, people can gaze through the thick sheet of ice to the water below. People snowmobile across the frozen lake and go ice fishing. In many areas,

For many Russians, a dacha is a place to relax, live simply, and spend time away from busy cities.

including the outskirts of the city of Yekaterinburg, people ride in traditional troika, which are sleds pulled by three horses. To warm back up, people move indoors for tea made with an enameled table-top hot water kettle, along with a variety of treats. These include sweet, crunchy rings of bread called *sushki*.

## UKRAINE

In the first few decades of the 2000s, Russia has frequently been in the news for its military aggression, including in Georgia in 2008 and in Crimea in 2014. Still, Russia's full-scale invasion of Ukraine on February 24, 2022, shocked the world. When the attack began, Putin told the Russian people that the goals were to denazify Ukraine and to demilitarize the country. Putin said he wanted to save the population from bullying by their own government. "It is not our plan to occupy the Ukrainian territory; we do not intend to impose anything on anyone by force," Putin told the Russian population.[2] He also blamed the United States and the countries of Western Europe for acting aggressively toward Russia. The Russian government called the invasion a special military operation and soon made it a crime for Russians to call it a war.

Contrary to many analysts' expectations, there was no quick victory for Russia in Ukraine. Ukraine had strengthened its military after Russia annexed Crimea in 2014, and the Ukrainian people showed a willingness to fight back. The Russian military's offensive toward Kyiv stalled, and Russian leadership eventually retreated

### SANCTIONS

When Russia invaded Ukraine in 2022, McDonalds, Starbucks, and Kentucky Fried Chicken suspended operations in the country. Restaurants that were not a part of international chains were also affected by economic sanctions. Marina Albee, owner of a vegetarian restaurant in Saint Petersburg, told a Euronews reporter, "We're waiting for the tsunami to hit—the tsunami being the price increases for everything we purchase."[3] Many foreign food companies no longer sold their products in Russia.

MINI **BIO**

# GARRY KASPAROV

Garry Kasparov was born in Baku, Azerbaijan, when it was part of the USSR. He first played chess as a six-year-old and was Soviet Youth Champion by the time he was 13. In 1979, he won his first international championship. In 1980, he became an international grandmaster. As an international chess player, Kasparov traveled more freely than other people in the Soviet Union. He frequently journeyed to the west, including the United States.

After the fall of the Soviet Union, Kasparov hoped the Russian Federation would allow democracy and freedom. But this did not happen. In 2005, Kasparov retired from chess to form an anti-Putin, prodemocratic movement in Russia. "This is not chess. This is not a battle between opposite colors, but of opposite values. Freedom, life, and love versus tyranny, death, and hatred," said Kasparov.[4]

Kasparov has remained active in the world of chess since his retirement from the game.

from the area, shifting their forces to Ukraine's east. With support from the United States and Western Europe, including significant shipments of weapons, ammunition, and supplies, the Ukrainian military put up a stout defense. Thousands of troops on each side died, and air strikes on Ukrainian cities killed many civilians as well. Millions of Ukrainian refugees streamed into neighboring countries.

Although the invasion was condemned internationally, support within Russia remained strong despite foreign sanctions. In one state media survey, 65 percent of those polled approved of Russia's actions in Ukraine. In another poll the approval rating was 71 percent. Alexey Bessudnov, a professor of sociology at the University of Exeter, told the *New Yorker*, "I don't think we can say that, on the whole, people in Russia love this war—that they like the idea of going off in search of conquest . . . we should

**During the invasion of Ukraine, Russian tanks were given markings, such as the letter Z, which may have been meant to help Russian forces distinguish them from similar Ukrainian equipment.**

remember what people have in mind when they say they support what is happening in Ukraine."[5] Bessudnov explained that the Russian government was tightly controlling what the media was telling the public about the invasion, with news channels reporting that it was a special operation against Nazis in Ukraine and not an invasion or war.

Some Russians protested the war. This was a bold move, as the government quickly cracked down on such actions. On the island of Sakhalin, a teacher criticized the war in her classroom. When the school found out, they informed the police, and the teacher was arrested. In the city of Tula, anti-war graffiti appeared in the weeks after the invasion. The police detained two men in connection with these messages. In one of the most visible protests, a producer on a major television news program stood behind a news anchor and held a sign reading "No War." The program quickly cut away from her, and she was fined for the incident.

## CHALLENGES

One modern challenge Russia faces is climate change. As temperatures warm, permafrost thaws, creating first impassable mud and then erosion. In Siberia, giant holes began appearing in the ground. Scientists discovered that these holes had once held pockets of methane gas. Methane is one of the gases that helps trap heat in the atmosphere. As Siberia warms and methane is released, the methane will lead to even more warming, creating a worsening cycle. Warming may produce some side benefits, such as thawing sea ice making more open ports available. But accelerating climate change will lead to climate instability, droughts, and flooding.

Another challenge is human trafficking, and especially labor trafficking. People from Asia and Europe are forced to work in Russia and pass through Russia as they are sold into slavery in other countries. In Russia itself, trafficked people work in agriculture, construction, manufacturing, repair, and domestic service.

In 2020, an estimated 794,000 people worked as forced laborers in Russia. Despite these numbers, only 14 cases of human trafficking were reported in 2018, and another six were investigated in 2019. Putin and others in the government deny that trafficking takes place in Russia. With approximately four million people migrating into Russia each year for legal work, traffickers hide forced laborers within the flow of migrants.[6]

Traffickers promise their victims high-paying jobs and the documents they need to work legally. The traffickers then withhold wages, take away travel documents, and abuse people both physically and mentally. Victims often refuse to help convict their traffickers because there is little protection offered to victims. Widespread corruption in police forces and politics also means that victims don't know whom they can trust.

### COVID-19

In the first year of the COVID-19 pandemic, Russia reported relatively few cases as the infection rate in many other countries rose dramatically. But as new variants of the virus emerged in late 2021, Russian case numbers rose. The country developed its own vaccine, called Sputnik V, but many Russians refused it. By June 2022, the country's death toll from COVID-19 was more than 370,000, and roughly half the country was not fully vaccinated.[7]

Russia's natural wonders, such as the frozen Lake Baikal, remained inaccessible to many foreign travelers while the country's war against Ukraine continued.

## LOOKING AHEAD

More than 24 million tourists visited Russia in 2019.[8] The most popular destinations that year were Moscow and Saint Petersburg. Visitors to Russia come to see Red Square, Saint Basil's, and the Kremlin. They come to experience the beauty of Lake Baikal, the forested taiga, and the country's vast frontier. Whether a visitor's interests are natural wonders, ballet, or cross-country skiing, Russia is a country with a wealth of things to explore.

In 2022, the future of such travel to Russia was unclear. Following the invasion of Ukraine, vacationing in Russia became difficult or impossible. Many airlines canceled flights to the country. The US State Department strongly urged Americans not to travel to Russia, citing the potential for the harassment or arrest of US citizens by Russia's security forces in response to the international situation. The department said, "US citizens residing or traveling in Russia should depart Russia immediately."[9] People interested in exploring Russia's rich history, stunning landscapes, and cultural wonders would have to wait for a return to peace.

# ESSENTIAL **FACTS**

## OFFICIAL NAME: RUSSIAN FEDERATION

### GEOGRAPHY

Area: 6,601,668 square miles (17,098,242 sq km)

Highest Elevation: Mount Elbrus at 18,510 feet (5,642 m)

Lowest Elevation: Caspian Sea at –92 feet (–28 m)

### PEOPLE

Population: 142 million (2022 est.)

Most Populous City: Moscow (12.6 million)

Ethnic Groups: Mostly Russian, also Tatar and Ukrainian

Religions: Christianity (Russian Orthodoxy and other denominations), Islam

### GOVERNMENT

Type of Government: Semipresidential federation

Capital: Moscow

Head of State: President

Head of Government: Prime minister

Legislature: Bicameral, with the State Duma and the Federation Council

### ECONOMY

Currency: Russian ruble

Major Industries: Machine building, energy, metallurgy, agriculture, chemicals, petrochemicals

Natural Resources: Oil, natural gas, aluminum, palladium, titanium

## NATIONAL SYMBOLS

National Anthem: "Gosudarstvenyy Gimn Rossiyskoy Federatsii" ("State Anthem of the Russian Federation")

National Tree: Siberian larch

National Emblem: Golden double-headed eagle with wings spread upward

# GLOSSARY

**BAPTISM**
A Christian religious rite that involves sprinkling water on someone or immersing someone in water.

**BIOME**
A community of plants and animals that adapt to and live in a specific climate.

**COMMUNION**
A Christian religious rite in which people consume bread and wine that memorialize Jesus's death.

**COMMUNISM**
A political system in which the government controls the economy and owns all property.

**CONSCRIPT**
A person who has been drafted into the military.

**DEFECT**
To leave one's home country to live in another, often in pursuit of a national ideology different than that of one's home country.

**FRESCO**
A type of painting done on wet plaster.

**HUMAN TRAFFICKING**
A form of modern slavery that involves the trade and purchase of human beings for sexual exploitation or forced labor.

**HUMUS**
The organic part of soil that is formed by leaves and plant material.

**ICON**
A particular style of religious painting.

**INFRASTRUCTURE**
The physical structures, such as roads, railways, and power plants, that make it possible for a city or nation to function.

**OMNIVOROUS**
Describing an organism that eats both animal and plant matter.

**PERMAFROST**
Permanently frozen soil that is characteristic of the tundra biome.

**SANCTION**
An action taken to punish a country or force it to follow international laws.

# ADDITIONAL **RESOURCES**

## SELECTED BIBLIOGRAPHY

Finlayson, Caitlyn. "Chapter 3. Russia." *Introduction to World Regional Geography*, 2019, worldgeo.pressbooks.com. Accessed 29 Mar. 2022.

Kim, Lucian. "The Dacha Is Russia's Summer Cure for Urban Life." *NPR*, 6 Aug. 2021, npr.org. Accessed 16 Apr. 2022.

Wachtel, Andrew B., et al. "Russia." *Encyclopedia Britannica*, 2022, britannica.com. Accessed 18 May 2022.

## FURTHER READINGS

Allen, John. *Debates on the Soviet Union's Collapse*. ReferencePoint, 2019.

Harris, Duchess, with Marcia Amidon Lusted. *Russian Hacking in American Elections*. Abdo, 2019.

Roland, James. *Growing Up in Russia*. ReferencePoint, 2017.

## ONLINE RESOURCES

To learn more about Russia, please visit **abdobooklinks.com** or scan this QR code. These links are routinely monitored and updated to provide the most current information available.

## MORE INFORMATION

For more information on this subject, contact or visit the following organizations:

**The Museum of Russian Art**
5500 Stevens Ave.
Minneapolis, MN 55419
tmora.org
Visitors to the Museum of Russian Art can learn more about the art, people, and culture of Russia through exhibits of photography, paintings, and more. Exhibits include contemporary arts, such as political cartoons.

**Russian History Museum**
1407 Robinson Rd.
Jordanville, NY 13361
russianhistorymuseum.org
The Russian History Museum works to help visitors appreciate and understand the history and culture of Russian people in Russia and wherever else they live in the world.

**The State Russian Museum**
4 Inzhenernaya Str., Saint Petersburg
en.rusmuseum.ru
The State Russian Museum, housed in a former imperial palace, contains the world's largest collection of Russian art.

# SOURCE **NOTES**

## CHAPTER 1. MEMORIES OF RUSSIA

1. "Red Square." *Encyclopedia Britannica*, 3 Oct. 2016, britannica.com. Accessed 5 Apr. 2022.
2. "St. Basil's Cathedral in Moscow." *Swedish Nomad*, 23 Mar. 2020, swedishnomad.com. Accessed 30 Mar. 2022.
3. "Moscow Population 2022." *World Population Review*, n.d., worldpopulationreview.com. Accessed 30 Mar. 2022.
4. Katie Warren. "I Rode the Legendary Trans-Siberian Railway on a 2,000-mile Journey across 4 Time Zones in Russia." *Insider*, 3 Jan. 2020, businessinsider.com. Accessed 28 July 2022.
5. "Trans-Siberian Railroad." *Encyclopedia Britannica*, 22 Jan. 2021, britannica.com. Accessed 30 Mar. 2022.
6. "Novosibirsk Zoo." *Siberian Times*, n.d., siberiantimes.com. Accessed 28 July 2022.
7. "Largest Countries in the World (by Area)." *Worldometer*, n.d., worldometers.info. Accessed 28 July 2022.
8. Alina Bradford. "Russian Culture: Facts, Customs, and Traditions." *Live Science*, 14 Dec. 2017, livescience.com. Accessed 31 Mar. 2022.

## CHAPTER 2. GEOGRAPHY

1. "Russia." *Nations Online*, n.d., nationsonline.org. Accessed 29 Mar. 2022.
2. "Russia." *CIA World Factbook*, 27 July 2022, cia.gov. Accessed 28 July 2022.
3. "Kamchatka Peninsula." *Encyclopedia Britannica*, 22 Nov. 2019, britannica.com. Accessed 6 Apr. 2022.
4. Kim Ann Zimmerman. "Mount Elbrus: Facts about Europe's Highest Mountain." *Live Science*, 1 Nov. 2013, livescience.com. Accessed 6 Apr. 2022.
5. Andrew B. Wachtel et al. "Russia." *Encyclopedia Britannica*, 23 July 2022, britannica.com. Accessed 28 July 2022.
6. "10 Largest Lakes in Europe." *World Atlas*, n.d., worldatlas.com. Accessed 6 Apr. 2022.
7. "The Tundra Biome." *UC Museum of Paleontology*, n.d., ucmp.berkeley.edu. Accessed 28 July 2022.
8. "Lowest Temperature – Inhabited." *Guinness World Records*, n.d., guinnessworldrecords.com. Accessed 28 July 2022.
9. Caitlyn Finlayson. "Chapter 3. Russia." *Introduction to World Regional Geography*, 2019, worldgeo.pressbooks.com. Accessed 29 Mar. 2022.
10. "Lake Superior." *Encyclopedia Britannica*, 19 July 2022, britannica.com. Accessed 28 July 2022.
11. Alastair Bland. "Lake Baikal and More of the Weirdest Lakes of the World." *Smithsonian Magazine*, 7 Aug. 2012, smithsonianmag.com. Accessed 28 July 2022.
12. "Steppe." *National Geographic*, 5 June 2011, nationalgeographic.org. Accessed 28 July 2022.
13. Wachtel et al., "Russia," *Encyclopedia Britannica*.

## CHAPTER 3. PLANTS AND ANIMALS

1. Jeanna Bryner and Alina Bradford. "Reindeer and Caribou: Facts about Majestic Deer." *Live Science*, 15 Dec. 2021, livescience.com. Accessed 28 July 2022.
2. "Amur Tiger Facts." *Wildcats Conservation Alliance*, n.d., conservewildcats.org. Accessed 28 July 2022.
3. "Wild Boar." *Animalia*, n.d., animalia.bio. Accessed 8 Apr. 2022.
4. "Mystery of Siberian Freshwater Seal Food Choice Solved." *EurekAlert!*, 30 Nov. 2020, eurekalert.org. Accessed 28 July 2022.
5. "Saiga Antelope." *WCS Mongolia*, n.d., mongolia.wcs.org. Accessed 28 July 2022.
6. "200,000 Endangered Antelope Died. Now We Know Why." *National Geographic*, 29 Jan. 2018, nationalgeographic.com. Accessed 28 July 2022.
7. Sandro Lovari. "Saiga." *Encyclopedia Britannica*, 11 Oct. 2021, britannica.com. Accessed 28 July 2022.

## CHAPTER 4. HISTORY

1. Caitlyn Finlayson. "Chapter 3. Russia." *Introduction to World Regional Geography*, 2019, worldgeo.pressbooks.com. Accessed 29 Mar. 2022.
2. "The Russian Tsars." *Pilot Guides*, n.d., pilotguides.com. Accessed 28 July 2022.
3. "Bloody Sunday." *Encyclopedia Britannica*, 15 Jan. 2022, britannica.com. Accessed 28 July 2022.
4. "The Tunguska Impact—100 Years Later." *NASA Science*, 30 June 2008, science.nasa.gov. Accessed 28 July 2022.
5. "Research Starters: Worldwide Deaths in World War II." *National World War II Museum*, n.d., nationalww2museum.org. Accessed 28 July 2022.
6. "Sputnik and the Dawn of the Space Age." *NASA History Division*, n.d., history.nasa.gov. Accessed 9 Apr. 2022.

## CHAPTER 5. PEOPLE AND CULTURE

1. Andrew B. Wachtel et al. "Russia." *Encyclopedia Britannica*, 23 July 2022, britannica.com. Accessed 28 July 2022.
2. "Languages across Europe." *BBC*, 14 Oct. 2014, bbc.co.uk. Accessed 9 Aug. 2022.
3. Niko Vorobyov. "How Do Ukrainians in Russia Feel about the Crisis?" *Al Jazeera*, 11 Feb. 2022, aljazeera.com. Accessed 9 Aug. 2022.
4. "Russia." *CIA World Factbook*, 27 July 2022, cia.gov. Accessed 28 July 2022.
5. "Revelations from the Russian Archives." *Library of Congress*, n.d., loc.gov. Accessed 12 Apr. 2022.
6. Alina Bradford. "Russian Culture: Facts, Customs, and Traditions." *Live Science*, 14 Dec. 2017, livescience.com. Accessed 31 Mar. 2022.

# SOURCE NOTES CONTINUED


## CHAPTER 6. POLITICS

1. "St. Petersburg Population 2022." *World Population Review*, n.d., worldpopulationreview.com. Accessed 28 Apr. 2022.
2. "Everything You Need to Know about United Russia Party." *TASS*, 22 Dec. 2017, tass.com. Accessed 28 July 2022.
3. Andrew B. Wachtel et al. "Russia." *Encyclopedia Britannica*, 23 July 2022, britannica.com. Accessed 28 July 2022.
4. "Alexei Navalny Sentenced to 9 More Years in Prison after Fraud Conviction." *Guardian*, 22 Mar. 2022, theguardian.com. Accessed 28 July 2022.
5. "Russia." *CIA World Factbook*, 27 July 2022, cia.gov. Accessed 28 July 2022.
6. Kateryna Stepanenko, Frederick W. Kagan, and Brian Babcock-Lumish. "Explainer on Russian Conscription, Reserve, and Mobilization." *Institute for the Study of War*, 5 Mar. 2022, understandingwar.org. Accessed 28 July 2022.
7. "Russia," *CIA World Factbook*.

## CHAPTER 7. ECONOMICS

1. Prableen Bajpai et al. "Emerging Markets: The Parts of Russia's GDP." *Investopedia*, 24 Mar. 2022, investopedia.com. Accessed 27 Apr. 2022.
2. "Russia." *OEC*, 2022, oec.world. Accessed 9 Aug. 2022.
3. "Fuel and Energy Complex, Industry of Russia." *Advantour*, n.d., advantour.com. Accessed 15 Apr. 2022.
4. "Industry, Economy of Russia." *Advantour*, n.d., advantour.com. Accessed 31 Mar. 2022.
5. "Agriculture, Industry of Russia." *Advantour*, n.d., advantour.com. Accessed 9 Aug. 2022.
6. "Agribusiness." *Russia Country Commercial Guide*, 15 Oct. 2021, trade.gov. Accessed 28 July 2022.
7. Cameron Abadi. "The Fall and Rise of the Russian Ruble." *Foreign Policy*, 8 Apr. 2022, foreignpolicy.com. Accessed 14 Apr. 2022.
8. "Convert Russian Rubles to US Dollars." *XE*, 2022, xe.com. Accessed 28 July 2022.
9. "Transportation in Russia." *Facts and Details*, May 2016, factsanddetails.com. Accessed 28 July 2022.
10. "Russia." *CIA World Factbook*, 27 July 2022, cia.gov. Accessed 28 July 2022.

## CHAPTER 8. RUSSIA TODAY

1. "Russia." *CIA World Factbook*, 27 July 2022, cia.gov. Accessed 28 July 2022.
2. Paul Kirby. "Why Has Russia Invaded Ukraine and What Does Putin Want?" *BBC*, 14 Apr. 2022, bbc.com. Accessed 16 Apr. 2022.
3. Naira Davlashyan et al. "How Are Sanctions Impacting Everyday Life in Russia?" *Euro News*, 11 Mar. 2022, euronews.com. Accessed 28 July 2022.
4. Garry Kasparov. "Stand with Ukraine in the Fight against Evil." *TED Talks*, Apr. 2022, ted.com. Accessed 16 Apr. 2022.
5. Joshua Yaffa. "Why Do So Many Russians Say They Support War in Ukraine?" *New Yorker*, 29 Mar. 2022, newyorker.com. Accessed 16 Apr. 2022.
6. Leah Waid. "Human Trafficking: The Secret to Putin's Economy." *Harvard International Review*, 25 Nov. 2020, hir.harvard.edu. Accessed 28 July 2022.
7. "Russia." *Johns Hopkins Coronavirus Resource Center*, 2022, coronavirus.jhu.edu. Accessed 28 July 2022.
8. "Tourism in Russia." *WorldData*, n.d., worlddata.info. Accessed 28 July 2022.
9. "Russia Travel Advisory." *US Department of State*, 19 July 2022, travel.state.gov. Accessed 28 July 2022.

# INDEX

# ABOUT THE **AUTHOR**

## SUE BRADFORD EDWARDS

Sue Bradford Edwards took a class in Russian history when she was in high school and has read about the country ever since. She is a Missouri nonfiction author who writes about culture and history, including the history of ancient peoples. She is the author of 21 other titles from Abdo Publishing, including *Ancient Maya*, *Hidden Human Computers*, and *Cancel Culture*.